# *POEMS*

# POEMS

by

POEMS



Published
in Miami Beach, Florida
United States of America
by
Pub Co #1 LLC

Library of Congress Control Number: 2018935794
Valentine, James
POEMS
1. Poetry
1st Edition

POE000000 **POETRY** / General

ISBN: 978-1-946997-02-9

# TABLE OF CONTENTS

# FOREWARD

## POETRY versus FREE VERSE

In addition to my poetry and lyrics, all of which have set meters and rhyme schemes, I write a little free verse. And although I love free verse, it's not poetry. I take exception to my free verse being called poetry, or my poetry being called free verse since they are two different processes and yield two different results. They both have rules which define them. They are not interchangeable. Free verse cannot have set rhyme schemes and meter patterns; poetry must. Free verse is free from poetry's constraints, which is why free verse was given a different name when it was created, to distinguish it from poetry. As though to deny that words have definitions, magazines like the New Yorker and "Poetry" Magazine erroneously refer to free verse as poetry and steadfastly use the adjective "classical" or "traditional" to describe poetry, as though they are trying to redefine the word poetry to mean free verse and require poetry to carry the moniker "classical" to be poetry! This is an absurd rewriting of the English language. In order to be poetry, the verse must be metered and rhymed.

Why then misuse the term? Writers of free verse feel neither inferior nor superior to writers of poetry. It's not as though they lack the intelligence or discipline or patience required to write a poem since a great deal of each is evident in good free verse. Both are "poets" regardless of whether they write poetry or free verse. All fill the definition of poets and artists as creative people with rich imaginations and powers of artistic expression. The first creators of free verse were quick to distance free verse from poetry, not in a competitive way, but rather to inform people of the marked difference between their exciting new art form called free verse and typical old poetry. They loved that free verse did not fit the definition of poetry and instead dispensed with set meters and rhyme schemes. Walt Whitman was happy in his freedom from rules he felt constricted his thought and expression. The results are writings which are very different than poetry. And yet certain folks persist in trying to push the misnomer "poetry" onto "free verse" which does not even want it, any more than bee bop would want to be called swing. Those touting the misdefinition of this unique art form, and thereby robbing it of its uniqueness, are not the writers of free verse, but publishers and promoters who I suppose think "free verse" is not good enough in some way! Why do publishers think that there's something so wrong with free verse that it has to co-opt the misnomer poetry?

Long ago magazines peddling subscriptions, and publishers marketing books, and promoters advertising free verse readings, all had a vested financial interest in passing free verse off as poetry because it's so much easier to use the well-known, age-old brand poetry than to build the new brand free verse from the ground up. Poetry has hundreds of years of brand building behind it. It's more lucrative to say that free verse is a "form" of poetry, though it is not. Free verse is not even an offshoot or branch of poetry; it's as different from poetry as prose. In fact free verse has far more in common with prose, yet we don't hear people calling it a "prose" reading, when free verse is merely prose split up into separate lines of sentence fragments. Business folks who don't even write free verse called it poetry in the name of almighty commerce, and it stuck. They scored a marketing coup as they shrewdly spewed their misinformation, and continue to do so to this day for the same pecuniary reasons, regardless of how illiterate it is.

The lyrics to my songs are not poems, even though they have set meters and rhymes, and are far closer to poetry than free verse. Even though my lyrics fit the rules of poetry, they are not poems, but lyrics. I could call them poems, but I'd be lying. They are poetic, but I would never call them poems because they are not. And it would have been far easier, more profitable, and more prestigious to sell them all as poems, just dishonest. See *Poems versus Lyrics* within.

Playing a sport without following its rules is not playing that sport but some other, especially in the case of free verse, which has no rules at all, and whose writers are the last folks to keep score, even though their publishers certainly are. It's the rules that give a sport its name, along with the dimensions of its courts or field, constraints of the type rightly and proudly discarded by free verse writers, who are running up a hill or taking a walk or throwing pebbles in a stream. Rules would ruin the activity whose entire point is to take a break from the rules and allow reap a different kind of reward than playing some game.

The rules of meter and rhyme give poetry its name, and following no rules gives free verse its name.

The limitations of poetry are antithetical to the freedom of free verse. While poetry writers must spend time having to limit their thoughts and feelings in compliance with the restrictions of meter and rhyme, free verse writers are free to spend that time considering the best possible feelings and thoughts without constraint, and are therefore able to achieve more accuracy of feeling and thought, and more freedom of artistry, by dispensing with the "artificial" limitations of poetry. In poetry one is at times required to delete a phrase or word perfectly suited to the poem just because it doesn't fit the meter or the rhyme! The process and product of free verse and that of poetry are completely different. Why then do so many call free verse, poetry? Is it laziness, greed, illiteracy, apathy? Free verse and poetry are two different forms of writing with two different names yielding two different results. One should not be called the other.

# PREFACE

## POEMS *versus* LYRICS

When I decided to compile this book, I considered presenting my lyrics as poems, because my lyrics have set rhyme schemes and meter patterns, and could be considered poems. But as I read through some of them, I immediately discounted presenting my lyrics as poems because poems are different than lyrics. Both delve equally deeply into feelings and thoughts, and require enormous amounts of time to contemplate those thoughts and feelings, and to solve the puzzle of rhyme and meter. Neither is more clever, more wise, nor more consequential. Both cover similar topics and subject matter. But they do so in different ways, and a reading of the two exposes a real difference, not one of form or substance, but one of style, the style of the language. Poems are stated differently and seem more weighty and profound than lyrics. The writing has more gravity and more magnitude, though no more capacity than lyrics. The difference is one of tone, and treatment of subject matter. Poems are more formal and scholarly, while lyrics are more straightforward and accessible.

Perhaps because poems must stand alone as an art form, they adopt a different tone than lyrics which are part of a greater work of art and are influenced by all the musical support and team effort that goes into creating a song. Poems must generate all of their substance, mood, and tone on their own since no other support will be forthcoming. Lyrics are supported by instruments whose job it is to accompany the vocal, while poetry readers are accompanied only by their moods. Musicians filling in around the vocals influence the feeling of the lyrics, which vary depending on the band or the producer, or by how the song fits an album or musical or movie it may be a part of. The vocalist must sing and the musicians must play within the sentimental constraints imposed by each other and by the producer and by the budget and by the product. Poems are like books and paintings and sculptures while lyrics are like screenplays. The screenwriter can rely upon both audio and visual support from sets, props, actors, and a soundtrack to bring the script to life. Songs and movies are made to be public and meant to be experienced by groups of people while books and poems are private and meant to be read alone.

Lyrics are sung differently by different vocalists while poems are read differently by different readers, both bringing their feelings and thoughts and past experiences to their interpretations, and adding the changes the lyrics or poem makes in their feelings and thoughts as they sing or read. Singers add feelings to the lyrics, to each line, each word, and even parts of words. Each singer has a different vocal timbre, and each interprets the lyrics differently. Readers add feelings to the poetry, to each verse, each line and each word. Silent contemplation imparts a personal interpretation to poetry as the reader listens to their inner voice and hears their own thoughts. In poetry, one has only silence and self.

# INTRODUCTION

## LOWER CASE and NO PUNCTUATION

I use the affectation of the lower case and no punctuation in my poems for reasons of design, deference and fairness. Poetry should look artsy and be easy on the eyes. The lower case give the poem a cleaner look than mixed cases. Punctuation marks likewise break up the smoothness of the design both within a line of poetry and at the end of a line which provides its own pause making punctuation unnecessary. Occasionally I use a comma within a line when required for clarity of meaning.

I also capitalize the word “I” because it pays homage to the solace of the reader, and looks too weird in lower case. But I do not capitalize “proper” names since not all of the people, places and things capitalized are proper, and may not deserve the compliment or reverence that capitalization bestows upon them. Proper words should have no prejudice over other words in an artistic environment seeking truth, but rather should have to prove their value like all others. Who decides which words should be capitalized and which not? Should God be capitalized but Allah not, or neither in case the reader may be an atheist? In emails and letters and prose and exposition, I follow the conventions, but not in art. Art should question everything. And a word like god still means God regardless of whether it’s capitalized. We all know what god means. Or do we?

I began using the lower case out of deference to the magnitude and resplendence of the Garden of Eden compared to my little creations. In spiritual and metaphysical practice, there is the concept of getting small to become large, of being small in order to get closer to the inner workings of sentiment by going unnoticed amongst those feeling the feelings and thinking the thoughts we poets plumb, or by listening to people pour their hearts out, allowing the small personal thought or feeling to become larger than anything in life but love.

# PROLOGUE

## POEMS

I wrote most of my poems from 1979 to 1985 when I was young and yearning to find my place in life in New York, Mexico, Australia, Singapore, Thailand, Hong Kong, China, Tokyo, London, Paris, San Francisco, Chicago and Las Vegas. With lots of character and plenty of principles courtesy of a mid twentieth century American education at the end of the hippy movement, and no guidance or mentorship from anyone, introspection and its expression came naturally to me. My exalted sense of purpose in a world of "might makes right" led me to wield the loftiness of poetry when it was the only weapon available to me in attacking who and what creates suffering. Truth was a saving grace in what turned into decades of philosophy and its practical application to the real world. Through forty years of intense and rigorous discipline, I steadfastly figured it out, and have these enduring poems to thank for aiming my arrow well at the outset of my flight to its target.

# cold

autumn whets the appetite
for the warmth of winter's mate
as the leaves which fall
compel us all
to avoid their dry light fate

sun becomes like candlelight
and the warm wind's backed by cold
as the fire which brawls
with the dark's brisk walls
winter black downs summer gold

# contented currents

I had a dream
about a lady
I love
but cannot have

she was a stream
I was a baby
above
lain in a raft

her sobbing tears
then raised me higher
I soared
but never sank

she was contained
as was the fire
which roared
along her bank

with her I'll float
until the ocean
of time
lets her escape

next to the moat
'round her emotion
she'll fine
my raft to take

# dawn through dusk

a day begins
and ends with dreams
a world of sins
wails in between
where power wins
by instinct's means
from empty bins
strong souls won't wean

a few men wheel
and deal all day
for sex, they feel's
not love but play
yet their game's real
their power's sway
an even keel
'no work, no pay!'

as children's toys
grow used and old
so adult's joys
are bought and sold
the market's ploys
some sell quite bold
yet what annoys
is life's so cold

the common man
not rich, not poor
with working hands

what he yearns for?
a roof, food, land
but nothing more
as hourglass sand
love's half his core

a beggar's life
a shipwreck reef
no work, all strife
he's been a thief
though passing rife
some feel no grief
a listless knife
cuts autumn's leaf

and beauty can't
be total truth
deceit's the slant
illusion's proof
and love is scant
where gold's the roof
so wise men pant
and stay aloof

a world of sins
wails in between
where power wins
by instinct's means
from empty bins
strong souls may wean
a day begins
and ends with dreams

# distant love

while working, friend
our minds would blend
we gained each other’s trust
and though too young
your beauty spun
a web to trap my lust

my body, heart
and mind did start
as different veins of coal
but when inflamed
were tamed and tamed
then, balanced, made love whole

I let you, love
rise far above
the pretty things you wear
the points and puffs
the tucks and tufts
the curves and black silk hair

our passion met
we felt no debt
but that our love survive
and neither slept
the night you wept
I left, our love alive

from then ‘til now
two times your plow
has turned my love from light
rainwaters flow
and strong winds blow
which land alone can’t fight

of my dim woes
o’er what you chose
in my stead unaware
as many are
until their star
starts tumbling through thin air

a heart thrice split
will not refit
such lavish love none dole
no lust's so long, nor friendship strong
nor's beauty reached that goal

and some demand
will foul the plan
'there'll be another chance'
but when life's done
our thoughts will run
to times of fine romance

illusion fades
with time's charades
our passion purely seen
I now construe
'cause overdue
to seem, at times, obscene

that men will vent
their lust's intent
towards you, provokes my fear
that one night cold
you might unfold
to one who'll later jeer

the comely men
and women end
right where they pass us by
the one night stand
as with one's hand
will show that lust does lie

if finally
again we free
the love which distance barred
I'll let it burn
the love I've earned
and heal the place that scarred

# elle

as you talk kind words are sought
but loneliness is hidden
you've been taught to add some thought
to what your heart has written

time amends what youth extends
such thought just might mistake it
don't pretend the past will bend
for weak love to remake it

how you long to love so strong
as romance would require
you belong as sunset's song
to memories you'll inspire

trust in love's security
satisfaction, purity

# evening I

as evening's last glimmer
steals light from the sky
a sliver blue shimmer
enchants weary eyes
and darkness grows dimmer
shades painted by sighs
our hopes now may simmer
our dreams now may fly

# evening II

a cascading camber
dusk's daily parade
as time's trusted banner
casts shadow charades
and symmetry scampers
through mute masquerades
while faith's wraith wears ambers
'til gilt becomes grayed

# figuras situados

driving hard through parching heat
on crowded two lane highways
colotlan, trizon, tepic
san juan, celaya libre
just names to me
a man who's free
in mexico one summer

diesel, dung and dust demand
attention to each mile
children tending tiny stands
do their time for survival
just scents and sights
but all too bright
in mexico one summer

migrants work a big man's day
though small and some are women
el jefe closely counts the pay
"it's hunger keeps them driven"
as day yields night
continued flight
through mexico one summer

wealthy children driving stoned
fast cars from cuernavaca
to the town their parents own
where others live as vaca
la ciudad
corrupt men nod
in mexico one summer

brand new buildings, stereos
signs of oil's new wealth
while in cardboard barrios
thousands die from ill health
the fixed façade
makes dawn seem odd
in mexico one summer

figures in a topia
serenely seek a new day
jorge, juan, alicia
laura, lupe, enrique
just name maybe
but not to me
in mexico forever

# fires

things we've kept
and those relinquished
tears we've wept
and fires extinguished

songs we've hummed
but wished were singing
hearts we've numbed
to love were clinging

# hauling

although my rhymes
seek stars sometimes
one coal can keep my fire
a woman's glow
or evil's woe
o'er my soul's rich desire

it's love I seek
on passion's peak
at truth's bold inquisition
where mystery ends
with fear which bends
from wisdom's imposition

I'm on the road
with faith's full code
and strong enough to crawl
through failure's caves
or over graves
of those whose dreams I'll haul

throughout time's jeers
I'll shed no tears
but closer push each hour
for though my guest
might short arrest
my soul will hold its power

# her eyes

her eyes were love
the size dreamed of
and full of salutations

they were the sum
of people from
all races and all nations

# labor's love

labor's love in his old heart
work's in order from the start
progress marches down the block
toward his building by the clock
still he takes pride in his work
pressing iron to each quirk

is his crime then to inspect
when in time all will be wrecked?

of our world what would he know
working scrupulously slow?
every wrinkle, every fold
could not tell what should be told
though his kind soon must depart
work's in order from the start

# liberty lady

my first love
my nurse dove
my thirst when she
saved me

her lithe style
her wise smile
her playfully
maybe

her slight frown
her white gown
her bright rays she
gave me

my youth's choice
my truth's voice
my liberty
lady

# lifecycle

it's so untenable
this blocked perplexing maze
we hear the clock
which ticks and tocks
between our acts on stage

and though ephemeral
our set untimely ways
we take to heart
each others' parts
in our long daily plays

# moky ryo

great black panther
feline lithe
with watchful wistful ways

less a dancer
more a scythe
for function from form fades

single lancer
single fife
makes motion march the maze

knows the answer
questions life
gives growth his gallant gaze

# my love slipped away

the morning was still
when my love slipped away
that night I felt chill
a void from decay

she'd leave before dawn
and I knew but regret
'til after she'd gone
my heart was beset

I slowly returned
to the room where we'd lain
consumed with concern
I'd dryly retained

then the door opened
to rejoin echo's plea
she had forgotten
to leave me her key

the moment was brief
but the kiss was prolonged
she felt my relief
redressing the wrong

the void still unfilled
I write on in dismay
the morning is still
and my love's slipped away

# nenekochan *(a)*

*(haiku)*

a child in the wind
her neck opened to the cold
a man she let's sin
doing as she's being told
not a woman but a mold

# nenekochan *(b)*

*(haiku)*

hourglass half full
a brief love overflowing
stretching with each pull
the young girl finally growing
his scarf where skin was showing

# plowshares

when everyone
can stand both small and giant
truth can lives infest

when none can run
defiance will be pliant
hate will have no nest

when choice is won
and conscience self reliant
love will take the test

# sun’s signal

life’s spirit chased
from stream to pool
new shimmer’s taste
like skin, can fool
though danger’s faced
and fortune’s cruel
forbearance wastes
towards air must cool

better mist than frozen be
like ice’s forlorn symmetry

so south honk ducks
and west honk cars
home’s warrior plucks
the skin from scars

but life, to me, must always be
the strife, the glee, of one who’s free

# the friendly day

is the morning like a person
who shows up every day
like the sun through weather's curtain
pulling us into the fray?

does "high noon" rustle and hustle
to get there by midday
in the middle of the bustle
so we stop to eat or play?

will the afternoon come find us
to see we have not strayed
to assure and to rewind us
then send us on our way?

has the evening been there for us
to soothe or sing our praise
to lead the sunset's chorus
in morals from our plays?

can the nighttime heal the psyche
get the moon to frown or jest
get the stars to shine so brightly
that we smile as we rest?

# the steps of truth

when ev'ry step has meaning
and's taken with respect
when ev'ry step is teeming
with love and care and zest

then ev'ry smile is beaming
and its light will profess
that ev'ry step is meaning
and each step is the quest

# the taste of work

I think I'll lie here in the sun
and taste the taste of work well done
I think I'll rest and breathe crisp air
and lose the thoughts which harbor care

I'll bathe in gold and doze on green
and view a blue which black redeems
I'll feel the diamond dew of night
come quench my thirst for love's delight

I'll share with stars stale stolid sighs
and whisper thoughts to fireflies
I'll laugh at time and cry in jest
and dream about some future quest

I'll stir, then wake, then feel the cold
and see the moon remaining bold
I think I'll rise now with the sun
and taste the taste of work not done

# this friend

a sand so fine
a water pure
an aged wine
a natural fur
an autumn sign
of winter sure
two things combine
and then allure

and how love shines
concern endured
as (s)he reclines
a bit demure
and casts his line
and sets her lure
this friend of mine
this friend of yours

# to the actress

you asked them all to feel
the love you know is real
thin applause
damned your cause
still you could not give up giving

though no one ever knew
you spent a long time blue
and you cried
and you tried
and your life has been worth living

# too many kings

when time and life and love are named
normal talk becomes inflamed
and common folk become as kings
who argue over kingly things

but what is time and life and love
to any who will rise above
the waste and death and hate of those
who wallow in tradition's throes?

it's fear and blood and pride's bright light
it's knowing what is wrong and right
it's grieving over bad acts done
by you and me by everyone

but what is fear and blood and pride
to those who have before us died
in times of hate from harsh decrees
by those who hold the kingdom's keys?

# torn tether

every time great people
rid the world of strife
they raise even feeble
spirits to new heights

ghandi was patient
walsea is bold
jesus was sapient
king fit the mold

you to something someday
might devote your life
if it is the last way
to exact your rights

then one day the tether
of love will revive
and we'll meet together
all of all mankind

latins and russians
chinamen too
buddhists and christians
moslems and jews

we'll agree on those things
whereby we survive
and with hope which trust brings
live the dream we'll find

# who else? *(a)*

who else can I laugh with?
who else is a treat?
who else should want me?
of all the who elses I meet?

who else makes me happy?
who else helps me sleep?
who else could have me?
while all the who elses must weep?

who else loves their lover?
who else wants their friend?
who else would be there?
after all the who elses pretend?

who else should I dream of?
who else could I know?
who else would love me?
to give all the who elses a "no"?

# who else? *(b)*

who else can I laugh with?
who else is a treat?
who else would I see?
inside all the who else's I meet?

who else makes me happy?
who else helps me sleep?
who else could smile?
whereas all the who else's must weep?

who else loves their lover?
who else wants their friend?
who else should be there?
from the start to the kiss at the end?

who else can I dream of?
who else can I know?
who else can I trust?
to tirelessly use the same beau?

# yet

lies look lovely set against the moon
but as we mine
the trace of time
they're evil faced balloons

boys seem lonely set next to a girl
then drawn to dance
pure pleasure's trance
stops pain but is no cure

I went so long
without a song
there was love in my pursuit
but no heart beat
on truth life cheats
so I'd stop to hear her flute

eyes shine brightly 'neath the dazzling sun
but without light
the mind's delight
will travel 'til it's numb

pools pend purely held by earth's full lips
but they don't blink
indeed they wink
when rippled by a sip

I strayed so strong
to sing my songs
and to get from girls a note
that as I leave
I, unrelieved
add to work the love I tote

# we did not say

where from here?
we did not say
love was near
life's softened sway
food and beer
a fun dismay
time would jeer
we'd let it play

truth we spoke
and bullshit too
fun we'd poke
as friends will do
I awoke
without a clue
time's trite joke
dawned with the dew

# MONTEMARTRE
Paris, 1985

On winter's steel nights, tall new symbols of corporate giants stress the flat incandescence of the city of light. Like a tall circus tent pole the Eiffel Tower props up the multi-dotted canopy allowing the Arc de Triomphe to blend in while older landmarks, like Notre Dame, lurk below. Away from this central setting, above the glitter of Pigalle and beyond the reach of the industrious hands of modern time, the city's only hill punctures the canopy displaying a portion of old Paris crowned by an enchanting domed cathedral. Watching serenely over the city like a grandmother rocking an infant in her arms, the Sacré-Cœur de Montmartre relaxes in the warmth of a yellowed-white shawl of soft luminescence. Mild, like the melancholy of Millet, and distant, like the devotion of Degas, she beckons the present with a whisper from the past.

Preserved on Montmartre's mellow folds is an aged little world cloaked in the colors of Corot and poised in the patterns of Pissarro. Stout cottages tightly packed in crooked rows confine the decadent undulations of a maze of narrow cobblestone streets which spread out deceptively as slope and effort quickly increase. Some of autumn's brown leaves linger in the dark soil of flowerless window boxes whose dusty colors and dirty tones complete a chromatic punctuation begun by the shutters and short doors. A crisp wind draws upward through these furrows of antique impression toward more curves, corners and streets sealed by the thin gray edge of a deep dark sky. A solitary stairway leads to a tiny park backed by townhouses and open to a view of the city below. Mysteriously thereafter, the slope then levels, and effort then subsides.

Towards the top, time waits for a nonoccurrent nod. Restaurants replace residences while activity assumes from gravity the duties of direction. In a small square, bare trees rise up through the cobblestones pointing their bony fingers to where the stars might be and propping up the neglected easels of local artists who sell portraits to tourists in the late afternoon to support more studious painting by daylight. One painter lingers, continuing to dab her palette in a crouch of concentration as she works from memory at a large canvas. Several restaurants provide the soft glow of light, the appetizing scent of cooking, the inspiring sound of music, and the warm chatter of people at play. Up the street and around the corner, the sounds of the restaurants vanish with the fading light.

Within the stout walls of a silent ancient yard, three life-sized statues hang on crosses among the black bark of tree limbs. Just beyond, the dark back of the Sacré-Cœur de Montmartre rests preponderate. Frigid moisture reflects the frontal light in rays which shoot back over the lofty dome and off the hefty sides separating defiance from glory and authority from amnesty. Worry slowly releases as the shadows peel away and her beneficent façade comes into view as tourists gaze enthralled. With a graceful glow warming her, the cathedral proffers charming testament to the harmony of the simple way of life.

## ABOUT the AUTHOR

Valentine sang his first rhymes as a boy tending the horses and cattle and working the fields and strolling the dirt roads that ran through his family farm near the Blue Ridge mountains and Shenandoah River in Virginia. In his teens he wrote his first simple poems for a mandatory high school poetry class. In his 20's he wrote most of his poetry, much of it well beyond his years, while modeling for Elite in New York from 1979 to 1981, in Sydney, Singapore, Malaysia, Thailand, Hong Kong, Tokyo, London, Paris and elsewhere from 1981to 1985, and in Las Vegas, San Francisco and Chicago from 1985 to 1987.

Valentine's world travels and experiences with all kinds of people in all kinds of work and play situations add a richness to his caring, feeling words. This is a guy who loves and understands people and it shows in his poems. Thirty distinct works cover the gamut of emotions and subject matter, each achieving sentiment as well as insight.